ASIAPAC

MW01075502

The Severe Code of The Legalist

THE SAYINGS OF HAN FEI ZI

Edited and illustrated by
Tsai Chih Chung

Translated by
Alan Chong

ASIAPAC • SINGAPORE

Publisher
ASIAPAC BOOKS PTE LTD
629 Aljunied Road
Cititech Industrial Building
#04-06 Singapore 1438
Tel: 7453868
Fax: 7453822
(as from 1 January 1993)

First published April 1991
Reprinted May 1993

©ASIAPAC BOOKS, 1991
ISBN 9971-985-57-8

Typeset by Pongrass Asia Publishing System
Printed in Singapore by
Loi Printing Pte Ltd

Publisher's Note

Legalism is a classical political philosophy propounded and practised in ancient China. It advocates a draconian legal code embodying a system of liberal reward and heavy penalty as the basis of government.

Today, through Tsai Chih Chung's creative illustrations, Asiapac Comic Series proudly presents you with *The Sayings of Han Fei Zi*. It represents the most complete set of thoughts in classical philosophy. Basic principles of legalism are forcefully argued and illustrated by reference to a myriad of historical anecdotes, many of which have become well-known Chinese parables.

We feel honoured to have the popular cartoonist Tsai Chih Chung's permission to the translation right to his best selling comics. We would also like to thank the translator and typesetter for putting in their best effort in the production of this series.

Asiapac's new corporate identity design

The Asiapac Books corporate symbol has its original inspiration from the Chinese character for Asia. The central globe symbolizes the international market for which we publish and distribute books, thereby helping to bridge the East and the West. The open book resembling soaring wings represents Asiapac, ever dynamic and innovative, aiming to communicate with modern society through the printed page. The green colour expresses Asiapac's commitment to go "green for life".

About the Editor/Illustrator

Tsai Chih Chung was born in 1948 in Chang Hwa County of Taiwan. He begun drawing cartoon strips at the age of 17. He worked as Art Director for Kuang Chi Programme Service in 1971. He founded the Far East Animation Production Company and the Dragon Cartoon Production Company in 1976, where he produced two cartoon films entitled *Old Master Q* and *Shao Lin Temple*.

Tsai Chih Chung first got his four-box comics published in newspapers and magazines in 1983. His funny comic characters such as Drunken Swordsman, Fat Dragon, One-eyed Marshal and the Bold Supersleuth have been serialized in newspapers in Singapore, Malaysia, Taiwan, Hong Kong, Japan, Europe, and the United States.

He was voted one of the Ten Outstanding Young People in Taiwan in 1985. He has received wide acclaim from the media and the academic circle in Taiwan.

The comic book *Sayings of Zhuang Zi*, published in 1986, was a milestone in Tsai's career. Within two years, *Zhuang Zi* went into more than 72 reprints in Taiwan and 15 in Hong Kong and has to date sold over one million copies.

In 1987, Tsai Chih Chung published *Sayings of Lao Zi, Sayings of Confucius* and two books based on Zen. Since then, he has published more than 20 titles, out of which 10 are about ancient Chinese thinkers and the rest based on historical and literary classics. All these books topped the best sellers' list at one time or another. They have been translated into other languages such as Japanese, Korean, Thai, French and Indonesian. Asiapac is the publisher for the English version of these comics.

Tsai Chih Chung can definitely be considered a pioneer in the art of visualizing Chinese literature and philosophy by way of comics.

Introduction

Little is known about the early life of Han Fei Zi apart from the fact that he was a prince remotely in line to the throne of the Han State, of the seven states of the Warring States Era (475-221 BC).

His name was actually Han Fei. The last character "Zi", an ancient honorific for men, was included in his name for the same reason that it appears in, for example, Kong Zi, for Confucius. Born in about 280 BC with a speech defect, Han Fei Zi was a keen scholar with a penchant for penology, law and statecraft. At the age of about 20, he went to the Chu state to study under Xun Qing, a renowned philosopher and thinker regarded as the Aristotle of China.

Xun Qing was a proponent of the view that man is by nature wicked and self-seeking, and control by means of moral education is needed to guide him on the path of proper conduct. It was from this school of thought that Han Fei derived his conclusion that man is intrinsically wicked but amenable to the rule of law. This conclusion was to be the cornerstone of his legalistic political philosophy.

Among Han Fei's classmates was Li Si, a native of Chu. The two men had little to do with each other until they met again in the court of the Qin state later.

Back home, Han Fei was foiled repeatedly in his attempts to get his father to accept his proposals for saving his native Han, which was weak and constantly threatened by Qin, its powerful neighbour. Frustrated, he channelled his energy to writing.

His thoughts were crystallized in 54 essays which are collectively known as Han Fei Zi, in his honour. This collection of essays is the most complete set of thoughts in classical Chinese political science.

In 234 BC, Han Fei was despatched as a goodwill envoy to Qin where his political views were held in high esteem by its ruler. Unfortunately, the Qin ruler's admiration for Han Fei was seen by Li Si – Han's former classmate – as a threat to his flourishing political career in the Qin Court. Li, conspiring with Yao Jia, a political strategist, convinced the Qin ruler that the brilliant Han Fei, if allowed to return home, would be a potential threat to Qin. Han was detained and forced to take poison in 233 BC.

Han Fei's legalist philosophy embodies the three main elements of *fa*, the law; *shu*, the art of control; and *shi*, power. At the heart of legalism lies the institution of a draconian legal code. The strategy in drawing up this legal code, he advocates, should be one which takes cognizance of the needs of the time and unfettered by a blind adherence to antiquated conventions.

In the broader interest of the state, the inherent self-seeking nature of the people should be exploited by a system of liberal reward and heavy penalty. This system, equitably and rigorously applied, should satisfy the people's profit motive, and simultaneously ensure the effective enforcement of prohibitions.

As an art of control, he also advocates a system of promotion based strictly on the law wherein every official is to adhere strictly to his scope of duty. An awesome display of authority which makes the people bow to the law, he argues, holds the key to social order. In external diplomacy, too, a superior position of strength gives the state the clout of initiative. Hence the emphasis on military and economic superiority.

To be sure, some of Han Fei's ideas and principles are tainted with personal bias and bigotry and unlikely to be accpetable in modern polity. For example, his doctrine of dictatorship and high-handedness is contrary to the concept of modern democracy. Nevertheless, many of his precepts, like all men are equal before the law, and the use of merit as the sole criterion of appraisal, are still relevant in the context of present-day government.

Alan Chong

Alan Chong, a former journalist, is a freelance translator and writer.

Contents

The Life
Of
Han Fei Zi

The Life of Han Fei Zi

1 Han Fei Zi, a prince of the Han State during the final years of the Warring States Era, was fond of studying the art of law application and statecraft.

2 He became a student of Xun Qing, a great scholar of the Chu State. Li Si, a fellow student, considered himself inferior to Han Fei Zi.

3 The Han State, the weakest among the Seven Warring States, was constantly threatened by the Qin State, its powerful neighbour.

4 The King of Han was feeble. Control of the state was very much in the hands of rapacious ministers.

5 The country will fall any time if nothing is done about its internal and external threats.

6 Han remonstrated repeatedly with the king and outlined remedial measures for national salvation.

7 You and your great ideas! Mind your stammer first!

8 All his efforts at national salvation were foiled by powerful ministers and the noble.

So he turned to writing, crystallising his thoughts in such works as Solitary Indignation, Five Vermin, Inner and Outer Congeries of Saying, Collected Persuasions and Difficulties in Way of Persuasion, which altogether covered upwards of 100,000 words.

9

Meanwhile, Li Si had become a trusted aide of the King of Qin. One day, after reading Solitary Indignation and Five Vermin, the Qin ruler exclaimed:

Superb! Must be the works of some ancient author.

10

16

The Philosophy of Han Fei Zi

Strict Adherence to One's Post

1. Once, Marquis Zhao of Han was drunk and fell asleep.

2. The crown-keeper covered him with a robe lest he might catch a chill.

Who covered me with the robe?

3. The crown-keeper, Your Majesty.

4. Marquis Zhao punished both.

As coat-keeper, you're guilty of neglect of your duty; and as crown-keeper, you've overstepped your duty. So both of you deserve punishment.

The sovereign's ruling principle calls for a strict adherence to one's duty, allowing neither overstepping of one's position to secure merit nor understating of one's performance capacity.

Fangs and Claws

1. The tiger can menace people and animals because it has sharp fangs and claws.

Help!

2. But not when it has lost them.

A clawless and toothless tiger is nothing frightening.

3. The powers of reward and punishment are the sovereign's fangs and claws.

Punishment

Reward

4. A sovereign who reliquishes his authority is like a subdued tiger at the mercy of the one who gains it.

A sovereign who delegates too much power to his vassals invariably meets with a tragic end and ruins his kingdom.

21

Kindness Begets Suspicion

A section of the enclosing wall of a rich man in Song crumbled during a storm.

Sages Know No Shame

Vanquished, King Gou Jian of Yue served King Fu Cha of Wu, heralding the way for his conqueror.

1

2

In the end, he could avenge his defeat and kill Fu Cha at Gusu.

3

King Wen of Zhou showed no sign of grief and indignation when he was held prisoner at the Jade Gate by King Zhou of Shang.

This paved the way for his son, King Wu, to destroy King Zhou at Muye eventually.

4

To Gou Jian, who emerged the hegemon, serving Fu Cha was no regret. Neither did King Wu, who gained the world, consider it a shame that his father was once taken prisoner. Hence Lao Zi's saying: "Sages know no shame because they don't regard shame as shame."

An Amazing Cry

1. King Zhuang of Chu, for three years after ascending the throne, didn't issue any decree nor actively conduct the state affairs.

2. The Right Commissioner of the Army said to him:

A big bird has descended on the southern hill. For three years it has neither flown nor sung but remained silent. What kind of bird is that?

3. It hasn't fluttered for three years to grow its wings; it has neither flown nor sung to observe the people.

4. Though it hasn't flown, once it takes to the air, it'll soar high up into the sky; though it hasn't sung, once it starts singing, it'll amaze the world.

5

Thank you, Your Majesty.

Don't you worry. I've got your message.

6 Half a year later, King Zhuang began to administer the state affairs personally. He abrogated ten practices, instituted nine measures, executed five ministers and secured the services of six able recluses. Immediately, the state became very orderly.

7 His troops invaded and conquered the states of Qi and Jin.

8 At Song, where he called a conference of the feudal lords, he attained hegemony.

King Zhuang never did good in a small way, nor reveal his intention prematurely, wherefore he accomplished a great achievement. Hence Lao Zi's saying: "The largest vessel becomes complete slowly, the loudest sound is rarely heard."

The Secret of Winning

1. King Xiang of Zhao learned driving from Wang Liang. Soon, they had a race. Three times Xiang changed his horses but thrice he lagged behind Wang.

2. It's obvious that you didn't teach me everything.

I taught you all the techniques but you applied them wrongly.

3. The most important thing in driving is to unite the horses and the chariot; the mind of the driver, too, must be in unison with the motion of the horses.

4. During the race, you were bent on overtaking me and were preoccupied with whether I was ahead of or behind you. Your mind went out of step with the strides of the horses, that's why you lost.

The secret of winning lies in concentration. A unity of the mind, the body and the task at hand ensures the best result.

The Wisdom of King Wen

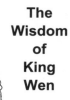

Panel 1

King Wen of Zhou had a jade plate. King Zhou of Shang sent Jiao Li, a worthy man, to ask for it but was refused.

Sorry, I can't give it to you.

Panel 2

Next, King Zhou sent Fei Zhong, an unworthy man, and King Wen acceded to his request.

My pleasure!

Panel 3

Unworthy

Worthy

King Wen didn't want a worthy man to advance his career under King Zhou, so he gave the jade plate to Fei Zhong.

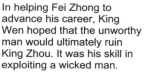

Panel 4

King Wen entreated Taigong Wang at the bank of the Wei River to serve him as military adviser. It was his skill in using a worthy man.

Panel 5

In helping Fei Zhong to advance his career, King Wen hoped that the unworthy man would ultimately ruin King Zhou. It was his skill in exploiting a wicked man.

He who doesn't esteem the worthy nor draw lessons from the unworthy, though he thinks he is knowledgeable, is actually confused and foolish.

32

Skilful Deception and Clumsy Sincerity

1. Yue Yang, a general of Wei, led an attack on Zhongshan. His son was in the besieged town.

2. General! The King of Zhongshan has cooked your son and sent you the soup.

3. Let me finish it and I'll flatten Zhongshan.

4. Marquis Wen, the Wei ruler, said to Du Shizan: Yue Yang ate his son's flesh for my sake.

5. He's prepared to eat even his own son. Who else wouldn't he eat?

6. Marquis Wen duly rewarded Yue upon his return after destroying Zhongshan but began to doubt his sincerity.

35

12 Qin was sent packing.

Three months later, Qin was recalled by Meng Sun and appointed his son's tutor.

13

Meng Sun's coachman asked in wonder:

Why do you do that after you've punished him?

14

15 If he couldn't bear to see the fawn suffer, would he bear to see my son suffer?

Skilful deception is inferior to clumsy sincerity. Yue Yang incurred suspicion despite his meritorious, service but Qin Xiba gained greater trust despite his fault.

38

The Likes of Fleas and Lice

1. Zi Yu introduced Confucius to the premier of Song.

Thank you, Your Excellency.

You're indeed a worthy man, Sir.

2. After Confucius had gone out...

How do you find him?

After seeing Confucius, you look as small as fleas and lice to me. I'm going to introduce him to His Majesty.

3.

4. After seeing Confucius, His Majesty will look upon you as small as fleas and lice, too.

5. So the premier refrained from introducing Confucius to the King of Song.

Vassals often refrain from recommending people superior to themselves for fear of losing favour. It's up to the sovereign to find way to overcome this so that worthy men are recruited into service.

Distant Water and a Fire at Hand

1

Duke Mu of Lu wanted his sons to take up offices in the courts of Jin and Chu. Li Chu remonstrated with him:

A drowning child won't be saved by good swimmers from Yue because they are too far away.

2

Likewise, water from the sea, though abundant, can't be relied upon to put out a fire at hand.

3

Now, though Chu and Jin are strong, Qi is our close neighbour. Will Jin and Chu be able to come to our rescue in the event of a conflict with Qi?

Practical usage counts. The best help is a timely help.

Holding up a Target for Yi

When Hou Yi, a legendary crack shot, got ready to shoot...

1

Even visitors from as far as Yue would scramble for an opportunity to hold up the target for him.

2

Danger!

However, when a young boy tried shooting an arrow, even his loving mother would keep a wide berth.

3

Even a stranger can trust another on something known to be perfectly safe; but a mother can't even trust her own son when it comes to a matter of little confidence.

Portent

A man had a cruel and fierce neighbour.

Finding the situation unbearable, he wanted to sell his property and move away.

The day of retribution is due for this guy. Why not wait for a while?

I'm afraid his day of reckoning comes only after he has killed me!

A portent of danger should be heeded and precautionary measures taken.

A Source of Courage

1. An eel resembles a snake and a silkworm, a caterpillar.

2. A man is frightened at the sight of a snake; a woman's hair stands on end at the sight of a caterpillar.

3. But the fisherman is delighted to grab an eel.

4. A woman shows no fear in picking up silkworms.

Motivated by profit a man would surge ahead, forgetting his abhorrence and fear.

Lice Fighting Over a Pig

Three lice were disputing with one another on a pig. 1

2 What are you quarrelling about?

We're fighting for the choicest territory.

3 The pig will be slaughtered soon as a sacrificial offering for the Winter Festival. What will you be quarrelling about then?

4 Thereupon, the lice stopped bickering and sucked as much blood as possible from the animal.

5 As it grew thinner and thinner, its owner decided to spare it.

Profit seekers, preoccupied with their own interests, are constantly in dispute with one another. If only they paused and thought of the larger issues, they'd realise their true position.

Wang Shou Burns Books

1. Wang Shou, a load of books on his back, met Xu Feng, a recluse.

2. Events are shaped by human actions which, in turn, depend on the exigencies of a situation. Therefore, to a wise man, nothing's immutable.

3. Books are born of man's wisdom. Therefore, a wise man never sticks to the letters of books. Why, then, are you lugging so many books around?

4. Thereupon, Wang Shou burned all his books and danced with joy at his enlightenment.

The wise do not keep books nor preach with words. They don't adhere rigidly to anything but follow the natural course of Tao.

The Double-mouthed Worm

1 There was a kind of worm with two mouths.

Crunch! Crunch!

2 Delicious! Delicious!

3 Owww! Oww! Hiss!, Hisss!

4 The two mouths fought over food and eventually bit each other to death.

Ministers who squabble for private gains will share the fate of the double-mouthed worm.

Bo Le Teaches Horse Appraising

1. Bo Le taught those he disliked to pick super-fast thoroughbreds,

2. And those he liked to pick ordinary horses.

3. Top thoroughbreds are hard to come by and yield slow profits but ordinary horses are fast selling and bring quick profits.

Geniuses are difficult to come by. The backbone of a nation is formed largely by ordinary, capable men. The sovereign who knows how to use these men effectively is a skilful one.

Gorge of Legislation

51

Taking Chances

Getting the People to Brave Fire and Water

In preparation for a war of revenge against Wu, the King of Yue wanted to test the efficacy of his training of his people.

Dong! Dong! Dong!

He set fire to a tower and beat the drum. Thereupon, the people rushed to put out the fire because there was a reward for fire-fighting.

1

2

He beat the drum by the river and the people rushed into the water because there was a reward for braving the water.

Dong! Dong! Dong!

3

4

On the war front, the people charged forward fearlessly because there was a reward for combat.

Dong! Dong! Dong!

If reward can make people brave water and fire, then the law maybe used to a greater advantage as a means of promoting the services of capable men.

Virtues are just for Jest

1. In play, children would take soft earth as cooked rice, muddy water as soup and pieces of wood as meat.

2. It's getting dark and I'm hungry. I want to go home for dinner.

   Grrr!

3. Eat these if you're hungry!

4. These are just for play; how can they be eaten?

   Hee! Hee!

   Eulogies for the legacy of remote antiquity are superficial no matter how eloquently they are expressed; and tributes for the virtues of former kings can't be used as instruments of government. They're just for jest.

The Art of Observation

Just Making Up the Number in an Ensemble

King Xuan of Qi loved the yu instrument and enjoyed performances of his royal ensemble of 300 men.

1

2
A bogus musician was able to stay undetected in the ensemble.

After the demise of King Xuan, King Min ascended the throne and he, too, loved the yu-in solo performance.

3

4
The bogus musician bolted at once.

A sovereign who listens carefully to individual opinions of his ministers is able to tell the wise apart from the foolish. This way, the incompetent will not be able to hide themselves.

An Acid Test of the Law

1

The King of Yue asked high official Wen Zhong:

Do you think the time is ripe to attack Wu?

Yes, Your Majesty.

2

Our people are ready because we have been keeping strictly to our words on liberal rewards and severe penalties.

3

Why not set fire to a palace building if Your Majesty wants to see the reaction of the people?

Good idea!

4

A palace building was set on fire but nobody came forward to put it out.

5 Those who die in fire-fighting will be rewarded the same way as those who die in battle; and those who survive will also be rewarded as those who defeat the enemies in combat.

Those who don't take part in fire-fighting shall be held guilty as men who surrender to the enemies in war.

6

7 Thereupon, men who had rubbed mud and ointment on their skin and put on wet clothes raced to the scene of the fire.

Liberal rewards and severe punishments, administered strictly, are effective tools to direct the people. Used judiciously, they're a guarantee for victory.

8 There were 3,000 fearless fire-fighters on the left and 3000 on the right.

Archery Justice

1

When Li Kui was governor of the Upper Land in Wei, he wanted every man to shoot well.

2

So he issued an order:

Any difficult case of litigation shall be decided by the outcome of shooting: he who scores a direct hit shall be the winner and he who misses, the loser.

3

Archery became a popular pursuit overnight.

4

In the subsequent battle with Qin, Wei scored a resounding victory because its people were well trained in shooting.

Man is self-seeking by nature. To get others to proceed in a desired direction takes nothing more than telling them the profit to be gained at the end of that journey.

Invoking the River God

He Bo the River God is an important deity. Why doesn't Your Majesty make an attempt to meet him?

A man said to the King of Qi:

1

Can you invoke him from the water?

2

Yes, Your Majesty.

3

4

An altar was set up on the river bank and the man started chanting:

Abraca-dabra!

5

At the same time a big fish was seen swimming by.

6

That's He Bo, Your Majesty!

Over trusting someone without consulting others makes one a vulnerable target for deception.

The Nature of Water and Fire

1. On his deathbed, Zi Chan, premier of Zheng, said to You Ji:

You'll be taking over from me after my death. Be sure to run the state strictly.

2. Few are burnt by fire though it appears frightening.

3. But many are drowned in water though it appears mild.

4. *You must set the law very tight and severe so that none will drown because of your leniency.*

Yes, Sir.

5. But You Ji proved to be too lenient. The country fell into disorder. Bandits were everywhere and gaining in strength. It was with great difficulty that You Ji managed to restore peace and order.

6. In remorse, he said:

I wouldn't have got into such troubles if I'd followed the advice of the late master.

Excessive benevolence undermines the law. If penalties are not severe and definite, decrees and prohibitions cannot be enforced.

The Crown Prince Is Not Born Yet

The Unburnt Hairs

* a legendary sword

Pebbles in the Bath

A Noseless Beauty

Monkey at the Tip of a Bramble Thorn

1. A man of Wei knew that the King of Yan had a passion for all things small and exquisite.

I can carve a monkey at the tip of a bramble thorn, Your Majesty.

Wonderful!

3. A man of great skill like you deserves a fief of 30 square li* When can I see your monkey carving?

4. Your Majesty must first abstain from the harem and from meat and wine for half a year.

5. Then, when the rain stops and the sun shines again, Your Majesty will be able to see the monkey in a dark, shady place.

Oh dear!

6. Hee! Hee! Hee!

That's too much for me!

* 1 li = l/2 km

72

7

So the king continued to provide for this man but never got to see the monkey carving.

I make carving knives, Your Majesty. The object being carved must be bigger than the carving knife. The tip of a bramble thorn can't even take the blade of a knife, how can it be carved into anything?

A blacksmith from Zheng knew of the matter and said to the King of Yan:

8

9

Your Majesty'll know the truth simply by asking the man to show his carving knife.

That's right!

What instrument do you use for carving the monkey?

A carving knife, Your Majesty.

10

11

Can I see it?

Let me fetch it from the guest house, Your Majesty.

And off he bolted.

The sovereign who doesn't take function and utility as the objective of taking counsel is apt to be deluded by spurious talks of roving strategists.

12

13

73

The Shape of Water

The Benevolence of Duke Xiang

1

The troops of Duke Xiang of Song were ready for battle in the Valley of Zhuo when the enemy soldiers of Chu were still advancing midstream.

2

Gou Qiang, Right Commissioner of the Army, said to Duke Xiang:

We're outnumbered by enemy troops. But we're sure to rout them if we attack now when they're still in disarray.

A gentleman wouldn't harm an injured person, wouldn't abduct old men of grey hair and wouldn't challenge troops not in proper battle formation.

3

4

We'd violate the principle of righteousness if we attacked now. I'd rather wait till they're ready before we beat the drums and attack.

A Dowry of Woe

1 Duke Mu of Qin betrothed his daughter to Zhong Er, a Prince of Jin.

I'll give you a grand dowry to add splendour to your wedding.

2 She was sent off with 70 beautifully dressed maids.

3 On arrival, the Prince of Jin loved the maids and gave the bride cold shoulders.

Ha! Ha! Ha! Ha!

Superfluity often clouds the real issue. The superfluous dowry maids from a loving father turned into a dowry of woe for the daughter.

77

Wooden Kite and Cross Bar

1 Mo Zi took three years to build a wooden kite. It broke after flying for a day.

2 The master is really skilful. He can make even a wooden kite fly.

My skill is no match for that of the maker of cross-bars for ox carts.

3 He can fashion a cross-bar with a short length of wood in less than half a day.

4 But the cross-bar can take a load of 30 dan* and last a long time, whereas the wooden kite I made in three years flew only for a day.

A refined skill without practical usage is worthless. One which can truly be called "ingenious" must be of concrete benefits to people.

* 1 dan = 45 kg

Raise the Candle

1 A man in the capital of Chu was writing a letter to the premier of Yan. As it was dim, he asked his attendant to hold the candle higher.

2

Raise the candle!

Yes, Sir.

3 So saying, the man unconsciously included the words "raise the candle" in the letter.

4

A letter from my master, Sir.

Fine.

5

Raise the candle? What does it mean?

Probably it means exalting the bright; in other words, elevating worthy men and appointing them to office.

A Diffident Governor of Shanfu

You Ruo visited Mi Zijian, the governor of Shanfu.

Why have you become so thin?

His Majesty appointed me governor of Shanfu despite my unworthiness. Work's heavy and pressing and I'm worried. That's why I've become thin.

Of old, Shun* played the zither and sang the South Wind Poem yet the realm was well-governed.

Now, you're worried governing a tiny place like Shanfu, what if you're to rule the world?

A resourceful ruler can relax on the throne while everything goes smoothly; but an unproficient one may exhaust himself yet be unable to govern well.

* a legendary virtuous ruler

A
Useless
Gourd

1
A Song man, Qu Gu, called on Tian Zhong, a recluse in Qi.

I heard that you, master, never depend on others for your livelihood. This gourd is a gift for you. It's as hard as stone and solid inside.

2
A gourd is valuable insofar as it serves as a receptacle. If it's solid inside, it can't be used as a vessel.

3
If it's as hard as stone, it can't be split and used as a ladle. Of what use will it be to me?

4
You're right, master. It's useless I'll discard it.

Tian Zhong doesn't depend on others for his livelihood but he, a recluse, is also useless to the state. Isn't he like the hard gourd?

Painting a Whip

84

A Taste of One's Own Medicine

86

Buying Shoes for Measurements

A man of Zheng took measurements of his feet before setting off to buy a pair of shoes.

In a hurry, he forgot to take along the measurements.

Shoes for sale!

Let me try this pair.

Very fitting.

I've forgotten my measurements. Let me dash home and fetch them.

Don't your feet give the best measurements?

By the time he returned to the market-place, the shoe-vendor had gone.

A sovereign who adheres blindly to the ways of former kings without regard for realities is like the one who believes in past measurements but not his own feet.

A Woman's Benevolence

Mrs Bu of the Zheng county was on the way home with a turtle she bought at the market.

Shao Shizhou the Honest Strongman

1. Shao Shizhou, a burly bodyguard of King Xian of Zhou, was an honest and upright man.

2. Once, after losing a wrestling contest with Xu Zi from Zhongmou, he recommended the winner to take his place.

3. Would Your Majesty please replace me with Xu Zi?

4. Why do you recommend him when you're holding a position coveted by many?

5. I serve with my physical strength. Now that Xu Zi's proven to be stronger than me, people will gossip if I don't recommend him to you.

When a sovereign recognises talents and use them liberally, vassals will not attempt to shield able men and all will emulate Shao Shizhou.

A Divorce of Public and Private Interests

1 Zhongmou had no magistrate. Duke Ping of Jin asked Zhao Wu:

Zhongmou is strategically important to us. I want a competent man to be the magistrate there. Who should I send?

The son of Xing Bo, Your Majesty.

2 Isn't Xing Bo your enemy?

3 Private feuds should be divorced from official matters.

4 Who should fill the magistracy of Zhongfu?

5 My son, Your Majesty.

Recommend the right man from among outsiders even if he's your enemy; recommend the right man from among your relatives even if he's your son. Merit alone should be the sole criterion.

92

A Father who Honours His Words

Expecting Repayment of Favour

1

Guan Zhong was held and being escorted from Lu to Qi.

2

En route at Qiwu, the chief guard accorded him great hospitality, to the extent of serving him food on his knees.

3

How would you requite me if by luck you survived and were taken into service by the king back in Qi?

4

If that happened, I'd take the worthy into service, employ the able and commend the meritorious. Why should I requite you?

How ungrateful!

When a sovereign's prestige ebbs, ministers should play safe by refraining from uttering upright words. Guan Zhong spoke forthrightly and incurred the displeasure of the chief guard.

95

Horses Can't Thrive on Empty Words

The Crown Prince is Not Above the Law

97

Qi Ruler Picks His Queen

1. Xue Gong was the premier of Qi when the Queen died. Ten concubines were in the king's favour.

Who's His Majesty's favourite?

2. He prepared ten pairs of earrings, one of which was exceptionally beautiful.

My pleasure to present Your Majesty with ten pairs of earrings.

3. So, this is the most favoured one.

The next day...

4. Accordingly, he proposed to the king to install the one wearing the prettiest earrings as Queen.

I concur with your proposal.

A ruler who reveals his likes and dislikes is apt to be deluded by vassals who adapt themselves to his wishes. Taking advantage of this ability they abuse their positions and thereby partake of the power of the throne.

The Principle of Statecraft

1

King Zhao of Wei said to Meng Changjun:

I, the King, want to act as a judge in deciding cases.

2

Why doesn't Your Majesty start by learning the legal code?

Of course, I'll start right away.

3

But he dozed off after reading a dozen pages.

4

These law books are really too much for me.

Instead of wielding the supreme handle of power, the ruler bothered himself with things meant for subordinates. Rightly, he fell asleep!

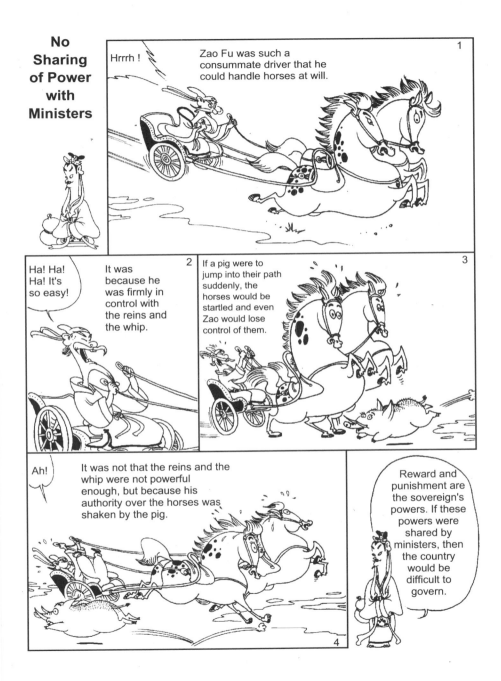

No Sharing of Power with Ministers

105

Profit's an Unreliable Means of Motivation

1 Wang Liang, another skilful driver, could drive horses without reins and a whip. His secret was to drive the animals towards places with rich fodder and water.

Give them what they like and they'll be at your command.

3 However, the horses would not respond to his commands when they passed by a vegetable garden.

Move! Move!

Crunch! Crunch!

Crunch!

4

It was not that the fodder and water had become unattractive, but because the horses were distracted by the lush greens of the garden.

A Cart with Two Drivers

1 Wang Liang and Zao Fu were renowned drivers.

2 If both were asked to drive a cart simultaneously in two separate directions, they wouldn't be able to go even ten li.

Go east!

Go west!

3 Tian Lian and Cheng Qiao were maestros on the lute.

4 If Tian played the upper notes and Cheng played the lower notes simultaneously, the result could not be any tune at all.

Even people of great skills cannot work together if they don't co-ordinate well. How then can a ruler share his power with his ministers in governing a country?

Incompatibility of Yao and Shun*'s Virtues

1

The farmers at Li Mountain encroached on one another's land. Thereupon, Shun went there and tilled among them. A year later, there were no more cases of encroachment.

The fishermen living by a river bank disputed over fishing territory. Thereupon, Shun went there and fished among them. A year later, they made concessions to the elders.

2

The potters in the remote eastern land made very poor earthenware. Thereupon, Shun went there and made earthenware among them. A year later, the quality of the earthenware there was greatly improved. Confucius sighed:

3

It was not Shun's business to farm, to fish and make pots. Yet he toiled so that the people would follow his example and rid themselves of bad habits. Hence the saying that sages teach by moral influence.

4

* legendary virtuous kings

Zi Chan Solves a Crime

1 While passing the quarters of eastern craftsmen, Zi Chan, the premier of Zheng, heard a woman crying.

Waa!

Halt!

2 Arrest that woman for interrogation!

Yes, Sir.

Why did you murder your husband? Come clean!

3 True, My Lord, I strangled my husband...

4 Master, how could you tell she was guilty?

It's natural for a person to be worried when a loved one falls ill and sorrowful when the loved one dies. I found no sorrow in the woman's crying but fear, so I knew something was amiss.

5 You're a genius, Sir.

Few crimes would be solved if Zi Chan had to attend to every case. If the law was made draconian and its enforcement as tight as a net all over the world, few culprits would escape.

110

Like a Tiger with Wings

1 It's said in the Book of Zhou: "Don't add wings to a tiger, or it'll fly into the village, catch people and devour them."

2 An unworthy man who gains power is like a tiger with wings.

3 Jie and Zhou, tyrannical kings of the Xia and Shang dynasties, were able to indulge in extreme lavishes and the cruellest of tortures, because they wielded absolute powers of the throne.

4 If they were mere commoners, they would have been found guilty and executed for offending the law before they could commit any atrocity.

Power, with its potential to corrupt and render a ruler as wicked as the tiger, is a scourge of the world.

Tripping Over an Ant Hill

1 There's an ancient saying: "One doesn't stumble into a mountain but trips over an ant hill."

2 It's because the mountain is large and easily seen whereas the ant hill is small and easily overlooked.

Big

Small

If punishment is not severe, people will take the law lightly. If criminals go unpunished, people will take to crime.

3

If offenders were put to death under such circumstances, it would amount to setting a trap for people.

4 Light punishment, like the ant hill, either undermines the order of the state or induces people to fall into a trap. Either way, it harms the people.

Waiting for Another Hare by the Stump

Long Sleeves are Good for Dancing

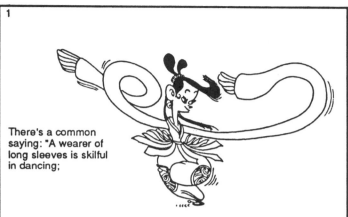

1 There's a common saying: "A wearer of long sleeves is skilful in dancing;

2 A possessor of much money is skilful in business."

3 Political reforms introduced in the strong state of Qin rarely failed despite being changed ten times.

Political Reform

4 In the weak state of Yan, however, even a single attempt at political reform failed. This doesn't imply that what Qin adopted was clever and what Yan adopted was foolish. It was just that conditions in the two states were different.

Political Reform

Resourceful people acquire skills easily. Likewise, a secure and strong state can devise schemes easily. The attainment of strength and security depends on an effective internal administration.

Asiapac Comic Series (by Tsai Chih Chung)

Art of War
Translated by Leong Weng Kam
The Art of War provides a compact set of principles essential for victory in battles; applicable to military strategists, in business and human relationships.

Book of Zen
Translated by Koh Kok Kiang
Zen makes the art of spontaneous living the prime concern of the human being. Tsai Chih Chung's illustrations spans a period of more than 2,000 years.

Da Xue
Translated by Mary Ng En Tzu
The second book in the Four Books of the Confucian Classics. It sets forth the higher principles of moral science, advocating that the cultivation of the person be the first thing attended to in the process of the pacification fo kingdoms.

Fantasies of the Six Dynasties
Translated by Jenny Lim
Tsai has creatively illustrated and annotated 19 bizarre tales of human encounters with supernatural beings, compiled during the Six Dynasties (AD220-589).

Lun Yu
Translated by Mary Ng En Tzu
A collection of the discourses of Confucius, his disciples on various topics. In this book, several bits of choice sayings have been illustrated by Tsai Chih Chung.

New Account of World Tales
Translated by Alan Chong
These 120 selected anecdotes tell the stories of emperors, princes, high officials, generals, courtiers, urbane monks and lettered gentry of a turbulent time. They afford a stark and amoral insight into human behaviour in its full spectrum of virtues and frailties. Glimpses of brilliant Chinese witticisms, too.

Origins of Zen
Translated by Koh Kok Kiang
Tsai in this book traces the origins and development of Zen in China with a light-hearted touch which is very much in keeping with the Zen spirit of absolute freedom and unbounded creativity.

Records of the Historian
Translated by Tang Nguok Kiong
Adapted from one of the greatest historical work in China, Records of the Historian, Tsai Chih Chung has illustrated the life and characteristics of the Four Lords of the Warring States in this comic book.

Roots of Wisdom
Translated by Koh Kok Kiang
One of the gems of Chinese literature, whose advocacy of a steadfast nature and a life of simplicity, goodness, quiet joy and harmony with one's fellow beings and the world at large has great relevance in an age of rapid changes.

Sayings of Confucius
Translated by Goh Beng Choo

This book features the life of Confucius, selected sayings from The Analects, and some of his more prominent pupils. It captures the warm relationship between the sage and his disciples, and offers food for thought for the modern readers.

Sayings of Han Fei Zi
Translated by Alan Chong

Tsai retells in his own unique style the basic ideas of legalism, a classical political philosophy that advocates a draconian legal code, embodying a system of liberal reward and heavy penalty as the basis of government.

Sayings of Lao Zi
Translated by Koh Kok Kiang & Wong Lit Khiong

The thoughts of Lao Zi, the founder of Taoism, are presented here in a light-hearted manner. It features the selected sayings from Dao De Jing.

Sayings of Lao Zi Book 2
Translated by Koh Kok Kiang

In the second book, Tsai has tackled some of the more abstruse passages from the Dao De Jing which he has not included in the first volume.

Sayings of Lie Zi
Translated by Koh Kok Kiang

A famous Taoist sage whose sayings deal with universal themes such as the joy of living, reconciliation with death, the limitations of human knowledge, the role of unpredictable and chance events.

Sayings of Mencius
Translated by Mary Ng En Tzu

This book contains stories about the life of Mencius and various excerpts from "Mencius", one of the Four Books of the Confucian Classics, which contains the philosophy of Mencius.

Sayings of Zhuang Zi
Translated by Goh Beng Choo

Zhuang Zi's non-conformist and often humorous views of life have been creatively illustrated and simply presented by Tsai in this book.

Sayings of Zhuang Zi Book 2
Translated by Koh Kok Kiang

Zhuang Zi's book is valued for both its philosophical insights and as a work of great literary merit. Tsai's second book on Zhuang Zi shows maturity in his style.

Strange Tales of Liaozhai
Translated by Tang Nguok Kiong

Tsai has creatively illustrated 12 stories from the Strange Tales of Liaozhai, an outstanding Chinese classic written by Pu Songling in the early Qing Dynasty.

Zhong Yong
Translated by Mary Ng En Tzu

Zhong Yong, written by Zi Si, the grandson of Confucius, gives voice to the heart of the discipline of Confucius. Tsai has illustrated it in a most readable manner for the modern readers to explore with great delight.

《亚太漫画系列》

韩非子说

编著：蔡志忠

翻译：张家荣

亚太图书（新）有限公司出版